PET CARE LIBRARY

Caring for Your Rabbit

by Colleen Sexton

BLASTOFF! READERS

4

BELLWETHER MEDIA • MINNEAPOLIS, MN

Note to Librarians, Teachers, and Parents:

Blastoff! Readers are carefully developed by literacy experts and combine standards-based content with developmentally appropriate text.

Level 1 provides the most support through repetition of high-frequency words, light text, predictable sentence patterns, and strong visual support.

Level 2 offers early readers a bit more challenge through varied simple sentences, increased text load, and less repetition of high-frequency words.

Level 3 advances early-fluent readers toward fluency through increased text and concept load, less reliance on visuals, longer sentences, and more literary language.

Level 4 builds reading stamina by providing more text per page, increased use of punctuation, greater variation in sentence patterns, and increasingly challenging vocabulary.

Level 5 encourages children to move from "learning to read" to "reading to learn" by providing even more text, varied writing styles, and less familiar topics.

Whichever book is right for your reader, Blastoff! Readers are the perfect books to build confidence and encourage a love of reading that will last a lifetime!

This edition first published in 2011 by Bellwether Media, Inc.

No part of this publication may be reproduced in whole or in part without written permission of the publisher. For information regarding permission, write to Bellwether Media, Inc., Attention: Permissions Department, 5357 Penn Avenue South, Minneapolis, MN 55419.

Library of Congress Cataloging-in-Publication Data
Sexton, Colleen A., 1967-
Caring for your rabbit / by Colleen Sexton.
p. cm. – (Blastoff! readers. Pet care library)
Summary: "Developed by literacy experts for students in grades two through five, this title provides readers with basic information for taking care of rabbits"–Provided by publisher.
Includes bibliographical references and index.
ISBN 978-1-60014-471-4 (hardcover : alk. paper)
1. Rabbits–Juvenile literature. I. Title.
SF453.2.S46 2010
636.932′2–dc22   2010011481

Printed in the United States of America, North Mankato, MN.
080110   1162

Contents

Choosing a Rabbit

Rabbits are smart, social animals. They make great pets! However, taking care of a rabbit is a big responsibility. Your rabbit will live for about 8 to 10 years. You must give it everything it needs to stay happy and healthy during its life.

! fun fact

A male rabbit is called a buck and a female rabbit is called a doe. Baby rabbits are called kits.

There are nearly 50 rabbit **breeds**. They come in many shapes, sizes, and colors. Some have long hair and some have short hair.

You can find a rabbit at a pet store, a **pet rescue center**, or a **breeder** when you are ready to bring one home. You will also need supplies from a pet store to properly care for your rabbit.

hutch

grooming brush

water bottle

Supply List

Here is a list of supplies you will need to take care of a rabbit.

- hutch
- bedding
- litter box
- nesting box
- chew blocks
- water bottle
- food bowl
- grooming brush
- rabbit toys
- rabbit food
- hay rack

Mini Rex

Flemish
Giant

Netherland
Dwarf

Setting Up a Rabbit Hutch

bedding

nesting box

litter box

Your rabbit needs a **hutch** to live in. The hutch should have a solid floor and plenty of room for your rabbit to move around. Cover the floor of the hutch with **bedding** and place a **litter box** in a corner. Your rabbit also needs a **nesting box** where it can curl up and be alone.

Make sure you check the litter and bedding every day. Remove any dirty litter and bedding. Clean the hutch from top to bottom once a week.

Place **chew blocks** in the hutch. Rabbit teeth never stop growing. Rabbits **gnaw** on chew blocks to keep their teeth a healthy length.

chew blocks

Feeding Your Rabbit

Your rabbit needs a water bottle and a heavy food bowl that will not tip over. Rabbits eat rabbit food and fresh vegetables. They are **herbivores**. Never give your rabbit meat!

hay rack

Hang a **hay rack** inside
the hutch and keep it full. Hay helps
rabbits **digest** their food. They need
plenty to nibble on every day.

Rabbits like **routine**. Feed your rabbit twice a day at the same times every day. Make sure your rabbit always has fresh, clean water to drink.

Care Tip

Pieces of fresh fruit make great treats for your rabbit.

Grooming Your Rabbit

! fun fact

Rabbits shed their hair once every three months.

Rabbits like to stay clean. They lick their hair to **groom** themselves. However, your rabbit can get sick if it swallows too much hair. You can help your rabbit by grooming it. Use a brush or comb to gently remove loose hair at least once a week. Rabbits with long hair need grooming more often.

Exercise and Play

Your rabbit needs regular exercise to stay healthy. Take it out of its hutch for at least three hours every day. Spend time with your rabbit while it hops around in a safe, closed-in area.

Rabbits love to play with toys. They like balls that bounce, empty boxes, and toys that can be dragged around on strings.

fun fact

Rabbits can jump 3 feet (1 meter) or higher!

Keeping Your Rabbit Healthy

Watch your rabbit closely for signs that it is sick. Take it to a **veterinarian** if it stops eating or is less active than usual. Your rabbit should see the veterinarian at least once a year for a checkup.

Rabbits are easily frightened. It might take some time to earn your rabbit's trust. Always talk to it in a calm voice and handle it gently.

Handling Your Rabbit

When you pick up your rabbit, place one hand under its chest and scoop your other hand under its rump. Hold your rabbit close to your body. That will make it feel safe.

Your rabbit can express how it feels. It clucks when it tastes something good. It snorts, growls, and thumps its feet when it is mad. If it clicks its teeth, that means it is happy!

! fun fact

Rabbits show joy by jumping and twisting in the air. This move is called a binky.

Glossary

bedding—material laid down as a bed for an animal; sawdust is the best type of bedding for a rabbit hutch.

breeder—a person who raises rabbits and sells them to other people

breeds—types of rabbits

chew blocks—wooden blocks that rabbits enjoy gnawing on

digest—to break down food so that nutrients can be taken from it

gnaw—to wear away by biting or chewing; rabbits gnaw to wear down their teeth.

groom—to clean

hay rack—a holder for hay; hay racks are usually metal and hang on an inside wall of a rabbit hutch.

herbivores—animals that eat only plants

hutch—a shelter for a small animal

litter box—a place where a trained rabbit goes to the bathroom

nesting box—a small, dark box where a rabbit can curl up and be alone

pet rescue center—a place that rescues pets; pet rescue centers care for pets until new owners can be found.

routine—a regular way of doing something

veterinarian—a doctor who takes care of animals

To Learn More

AT THE LIBRARY

Bodden, Valerie. *Rabbits*. Mankato, Minn.: Creative Education, 2007.

Miller, Michaela. *Rabbits*. Laguna Hills, Calif.: QEB Publishing, 2006.

Vogel, Julia. *Are You My Rabbit?* Edina, Minn.: Magic Wagon, 2009.

ON THE WEB

Learning more about pet care is as easy as 1, 2, 3.

1. Go to www.factsurfer.com.

2. Enter "pet care" into the search box.

3. Click the "Surf" button and you will see a list of related Web sites.

With factsurfer.com, finding more information is just a click away.

Index

The images in this book are reproduced through the courtesy of: Juan Martinez, front cover; Morales Morales/Photolibrary, front cover (small), pp. 4-5; Marilyn Barbone, p. 6 (top); Alexander Kalina, p. 6 (middle); Juan Eppardo, p. 6 (bottom); Ron Levine/Getty Images, pp. 6-7; Linn Currie, p. 7 (left); Caroline Vancoillie, p. 7 (middle); Wendy M. Simmons, p. 7 (right); Juniors Bildarchiv/Photolibrary, pp. 8-9, 17 (small), 21 (small); Mark Eastment, p. 10; J-L. Klein & M-L. Hubert/Photolibrary, p. 11; Juniors Bildarchiv/ Age Fotostock, pp. 12-13; PICANI/D Baum/Age Fotostock, p. 14; Katrina Brown, p. 15; Marcel Weber/ Photolibrary, pp. 16-17; Sean Locke, p. 18; Claudia Rehm/Photolibrary, p. 19; Daniel Bendjy, pp. 20-21.